JUDITH E. GREENBERG

HELEN H. CAREY

JEWISH HOLIDAYS

FRANKLIN WATTS
New York/London/Toronto/Sydney/1984
A FIRST BOOK

Illustration by Vantage Art, Inc.

Photographs courtesy of: Religious News Service:
opposite p. 1, pp. 10, 15, 24, 28, 34, 38, 42, 55;
Consulate General of Israel, Information Department: pp. 18, 50;
New York Public Library Picture Collection: p. 59.

Library of Congress Cataloging in Publication Data

Greenberg, Judith E.
Jewish holidays.

(A First book)
Bibliography: p.
Includes index.
Summary: Briefly describes the yearly cycle of Jewish
holidays, including high holy days, harvest holidays,
festivals, and modern holidays, with recipes and instruc-
tions for Jewish holiday foods and crafts.
1. Fasts and feasts—Judaism—Juvenile literature.
[1. Fasts and feasts—Judaism.   2. Holidays.   3. Cookery,
Jewish.   4. Handicraft]   I. Carey, Helen H.   II. Title.
BM690.G67 1985   296.4′3   84-20983
ISBN 0-531-04913-2

CONTENTS

ONE
*Jewish Holidays
Throughout the Year*
1

TWO
High Holy Days
5

THREE
Harvest Holidays
13

FOUR
Historical Holidays
21

FIVE
Festivals
32

SIX
Modern Holidays
45

SEVEN
Holiday Recipes and Crafts
53

For Further Reading
63

Index
65

FOR DR. JESHAIA SCHNITZER
*a man who loves children
and teaches them by gentle example*

1

JEWISH HOLIDAYS THROUGHOUT THE YEAR

Everywhere they live, people celebrate holidays that are special to them. Some of these holidays celebrate events that happen every year, such as the coming of Spring or the gathering of the harvest. Others may mark an important "first time." Sometimes the purpose is to recall an event that happened to real people who lived a long time ago. Or it may be a special day when people remember a turning point or an unusual achievement.

The Jewish holidays celebrate many of these same kind of events. But they also observe other events that mark their history as a people or are important to their religion. Many

This boy is holding the Torah, a scroll of the books of Moses, which describes many holidays celebrated in the Jewish calendar.

Jewish holidays date back to biblical times and are mentioned in the Torah, which contains the first five books of the Bible, the books of Moses. The Torah is a scroll, handwritten on parchment (paper made from animal skins). The Torah explains the history of the Jewish people and contains the laws they live by. Other holidays are as new as the state of Israel. In this book you will read about the activities that mark these important days. You will also learn about holidays that celebrate beginnings—the beginning of the world or religious freedom. And about holidays that celebrate endings, such as a harvest, the end of the work week, or the end of slavery.

This book is designed to increase your understanding of the Jewish holidays and customs and traditions that are associated with each. You will learn about:

The High Holy Days—solemn days of judgment
Harvest Holidays—celebration of crops and seasons
Historical Holidays—celebrations of actual events
Festival Holidays—celebrations with great festivities
Modern Holidays—newly-created celebrations

All of the Jewish holidays occur at specific times of the year, according to the Jewish calendar. The Jewish calendar is different from other calendars. The calendar you are accustomed to using is based on the earth's movements around the sun and is therefore called a solar calendar. But the Jewish calendar is based on the movements of the moon as well as the sun. The Jewish calendar day begins at *sundown* instead of the second after midnight, and ends the following sundown. If this is confusing, think of your birthday. Suppose your birthday is next Saturday. According to the Jewish calendar, you would start celebrating your birthday when the sun goes down on Friday evening and continue until the sun sets on Saturday.

In ancient times, Jews watched the sky to keep track of the new moon so they could tell when a new month was beginning. When the new moon was spotted, that day was called Rosh Hodesh, which means "Head of the Month." The people who watched for the new moon were stationed in Jerusalem, and they would pass the word to messengers who, in turn, traveled throughout Israel to tell all the people. The messengers traveled as far as fifteen days from Jerusalem in each direction. It took much longer to get the message to Jews living beyond Israel's borders, and sometimes these people might miss the sighting of the new moon. Their calendars would then be wrong and they would miss a holiday. To be safe, Jews outside of Israel began celebrating each major holiday for two days; in this way, they were sure not to miss it. Thus the tradition was established that Jews in Israel celebrate a holiday for one day and Jews living elsewhere celebrate for two days. Rosh Hashanah is celebrated for two days in Israel and only Yom Kippur is celebrated by Jews everywhere for one day. This exception is made because Jews fast on this holiday and it would be unhealthy to fast for two days.

Each holiday follows customs and traditions that tell the Jewish people how to celebrate. Families also develop their own ways to celebrate each holiday with special foods, songs, and crafts. The last chapter in this book contains recipes for some of these dishes and directions for crafts you can make yourself.

Jews have lived all over the world, and the way one family celebrates a holiday may be different from other families, depending on which part of the world their ancestors lived in. Most Jews have either a Spanish and Mid-Eastern background (Sephardim) or an Eastern European background (Ashkenazim). The recipes and crafts include favorites from both Sephardic and Ashkenazic families. Other differences may be found in the services for each holiday. Reform, Conservative, and Orthodox Jews celebrate all the holidays but some differences exist. Orthodox Jews follow the rules established over two hundred years ago. Conservative and Reform have allowed more modernization to account for living in modern times. For example, Reform Jews celebrate the holidays for one day, and the services are mostly in English.

This book tells about holidays that may be different from those you celebrate, but like holidays everywhere they are filled with joy and meaning. These holidays help the Jewish people understand their past, and this understanding helps them build their future.

2

HIGH
HOLY DAYS

About the time that you start a new school year, the Jewish
calendar is beginning a new year. The holiday that celebrates
the beginning of the Jewish New Year is called Rosh Hashanah. It marks the "head" of the year, which is an important
beginning. (In Hebrew Rosh means head.)

Rosh Hashanah is such a holy day that, along with Yom
Kippur, it is called a High Holy Day. These holidays are not
celebrated by parties or picnics because they are serious and
solemn occasions that require long hours of praying and fasting. The meaning of the High Holy Days, however, is important for all Jews. It celebrates the day that the earth was
created and is *not* a noisy, wild celebration like the New
Year's Eve of December 31. The prayers in the synagogue are
quiet and serious. They look at the way a person has lived his
or her life that year.

In the Rosh Hashanah prayers Jews ask God to "Remember us for life, O King who delights in life; inscribe us in the

Book of Life, for Thy sake, O God of Life." The word "life" appears four times in a short prayer. Rosh Hashanah is also called the Day of Judgment—Yom Hadin—a day to think of the year you have lived and promise yourself to do better.

While praying on Rosh Hashanah, Jews try to be closer to God and ask what God wants of them. In silent prayers and prayers said by the congregation, Jews ask how can they be better people, better Jews, and be closer to God. It's almost as if God is measuring each person, and Jews feel that they must try to see how well they have come up to meeting the standards set by God. Jews do not believe that God is trying to make them feel guilty so they can be punished. Instead, God wants to give them a new chance in a new year to become better people.

An important part of the Rosh Hashanah service is the Alenu prayer. Only on Rosh Hashanah and Yom Kippur do Jews bow down before God. On the High Holy Days they make a special point of showing they accept God as the king over all by bowing down during this Alenu prayer.

> We bend the knee and prostrate ourselves and make acknowledgement before the King of Kings, the Holy One, blessed be He, who stretched out the heavens and laid the foundations of the earth, whose glorious throne is in the heavens and the home of whose majesty is in the loftiest heights.

Along with these special and solemn prayers, Jews listen to the blowing of the *shofar*, or ram's horn. Blowing the shofar reminds the Jewish people of the story of Abraham and his son Isaac. In this Torah story, God tells Abraham to take Isaac to a mountain top and offer him up as a sacrifice. Abraham loved his son deeply and did not want to kill him, but he was prepared to do what God commanded. He tied the boy with ropes and prepared to sacrifice him. God stopped Abraham and told him he didn't really want Isaac killed. God had really wanted to test Abraham's faithfulness. Since Abraham proved he was willing to kill his own son, God knew Abraham was faithful. Instead of Isaac, Abraham sacrificed a ram, and the shofar is a reminder of this. The ancient Israelites used a ram's horn to call the people to attention. Today the shofar's blast (it sounds somewhat like a high-pitched foghorn) calls attention to the importance of the New Year and the promise to follow God's commandments. (The Hebrew word for commandments is *Mitzvah*.) To hear the "voice" of the shofar is a mitzvah.

On the afternoon of Rosh Hashanah, it is customary for Jews to celebrate with another special ceremony called Tashlich, in which they "throw" away their sins. They walk to a nearby river or stream and either empty their pockets or throw bread crumbs into the water. The purpose of this ceremony is to allow a person to begin the new year with a fresh start.

On the second day of Rosh Hashanah the prayers are repeated. When the services are over, Jews feel serious about their decision to be a better person in the New Year. They are also happy because they have given the New Year a good start.

Jews celebrate Rosh Hashanah by sending friends and relatives special New Year's greeting cards. These cards usually have a religious symbol or an artistic drawing on the cover. Inside are wishes for a happy and healthy New Year. These messages are written in English or Hebrew. People wish each other "Shanah Tovah," which means Good Year, or "Leshanah Tovah Tikatevu," which means "May God write you down for a good year," and which comes from the belief that God writes in His Book of Life at this time whether you have lived a good life that year. Rosh Hashanah, therefore, is a time when Jews are judged by God.

In their homes, Jews have a holiday dinner on the eve of Rosh Hashanah. They eat a loaf of bread called a *challah*. Prayers are said over the Rosh Hashanah candles and the challah. The challah is round in shape to represent a full round year. Family members wish one another a happy New Year by dipping a piece of challah into honey and then eating it. This represents a fruitful and sweet new year.

YOM KIPPUR

Rosh Hashanah begins a period of ten days that Jews call the Days of Awe. During these ten days of Awe, Jews think about the year that has passed. Have they hurt someone, committed a sin, forgotten God, or acted in any other wrong manner? The last of these days is Yom Kippur. On the day of Yom Kippur Jewish people ask to be forgiven for any wrongdoing. It is not enough to ask just for themselves. A Jew asks forgiveness for the whole community so that no wrong is missed or forgotten.

Before this very long holy day begins, a huge meal is eaten. It must be finished before sundown as Jews fast for the entire twenty-four hours of Yom Kippur. This means that no food or drink is allowed for a whole day. Fasting is difficult, but it is not supposed to be an easy task as Yom Kippur requires very serious and hard thinking. Fasting helps to clear the thoughts and open a person's mind to the prayers and need for forgiveness. These Yom Kippur prayers are the most important of the year.

At sundown, Yom Kippur begins with the *Kol Nidre* service. The name of this evening service comes from the Kol Nidre prayer in which Jews ask God's forgiveness for all the promises they make to Him and do not keep. The prayer is sung by the cantor, three times, getting louder each time. It is a very beautiful prayer. For Yom Kippur, the rabbi and cantor dress in white. (The cantor is the person who leads the congregation in prayers.) Many members of the congregation also wear white although it is not required. Wearing white is a tradition because white represents forgiveness.

On the day of Yom Kippur the services are very long, usually lasting from early morning until sundown. Many prayers are said, asking for forgiveness. The services also include a special set of prayers to remember loved ones who have died. This memorial service is called *Yahrzeit*.

Children are not expected to participate in a whole day of prayer, fasting, and serious thought. Instead, many synagogues have a separate children's service that is often led by a teacher from the congregation's Sunday or religious school. Although children who are under thirteen years of age do not have to fast, they can learn the meaning of being sorry and praying with sincerity. They learn this through stories that teach by example. The following story is one that is commonly told. This old but still popular story helps young people understand the meaning of blowing the shofar.

A great rabbi, the Maggid of Dubna, long ago tried to help children understand the importance of hearing the shofar's blast and understand its meaning with the following story:

"A country peasant once happened to come into town just when a great fire had broken out. He saw people standing and blowing trumpets in the town square. All the townspeople came running with axes and shovels and pails and

On the High Holy Days of Rosh Hashanah and
Yom Kippur the rabbi blows the ram's horn,
the shofar, to remind Jews of the greatness of God.

buckets. The peasant stood there thinking that these city people were very strange. As he saw it, when there's a fire, the people form a musical band in the middle of the town square to blow trumpets and beat drums. Are they celebrating having a fire, he wondered?

"A resident of the town explained. The drum-beating and the trumpeting were for the purpose of putting out the fire. The peasant was amazed at this wonderful idea. He went into a shop and bought a large drum and took it back with him to his village so he could put out any fires there.

"Sure enough, not long after he returned to his home, a fire broke out in his village and the people gathered to put out the fire. He called out to everyone: 'Don't bother doing anything. I have brought back something from the city which will chase away the flames and put out the fire.'

"He took the drum, and standing in front of the burning house, he beat on the drum with all his might. Oh, no! The more he banged on the drum, the more fire spread. Finally the crowd started shouting at him. 'Idiot!' they cried, 'You can't put out a fire by just beating on your drum. The drum is only meant to alarm the people of the village so they can come and stop the fire and save themselves and their neighbors.'

"And thus," concluded the rabbi, "so it is with the hearing of the shofar. It calls attention to the need to humble oneself before the greatness of God, to repent, or feel sorry for past wrongs, and to prepare to do something good for one's fellow people. But the people themselves must do the work."

All Jews should hear the shofar blown on Rosh Hashanah and Yom Kippur. However, hearing it is not enough. The hearer must also understand its meaning. The shofar calls attention to the need to humble oneself before the greatness of God, to repent, or feel sorry for past wrongs, and to prepare to do something good for one's fellow people.

Children aren't the only ones who are excused from fasting on Yom Kippur. Since fasting is not meant to punish or hurt anyone, other exceptions to the fasting rule can be made. Sick people, pregnant women, and very old people could be harmed or made ill by fasting, so they must eat.

This long day is filled with deep emotion and makes the people very tired. At the same time they feel good about themselves.

The last part of the day is the *Neilah* service, which closes Yom Kippur. The shofar is sounded one last time. The days of Awe and Yom Kippur are over. As they leave the synagogue, Jewish people wish their friends and family a *Shenah Tovah*, a "Good Year."

Now most people go home and have a meal of light foods to break or end their fast. Sometimes many relatives will gather at one home and have a quiet party to break their fast. Menus usually include foods that are like breakfast: eggs, fruit, pastries, and salads. Family members and friends share a happy meal trusting that God has forgiven each one for his or her sins.

Since the whole day has given each person an opportunity to make right any wrongs that he or she may have done that year, Yom Kippur is also known as the Day of Atonement.

Rosh Hashanah and Yom Kippur occur in the fall of each year. They begin a New Year that is filled with many special days. Throughout this year, these holidays deal with a lasting theme of Jewish history—the contact between Jewish people and God. Of all of these holidays, however, none are as solemn as the High Holy Days.

3

HARVEST
HOLIDAYS

The Jewish harvest holidays have their roots in ancient cere-
monies having to do with the land. Many of the symbols
used in celebrating these holidays today serve to remind
Jews of their ancestors' struggle to grow and harvest their
crops and to survive in a land with more than enough sun
and not enough water.

SUKKOTH

Like Rosh Hashanah and Yom Kippur, Sukkoth is a fall holiday. It celebrates the harvest of foods that have grown all
summer, and in that sense it is similar to the American holiday of Thanksgiving. Americans give thanks for the nourish-
ing crops that helped the Pilgrims survive and enabled the
community to grow. Today, Thanksgiving is a time when
Americans give thanks for the many things they share. It is
also the time when we are reminded of the bounty American
farms provide, for which we are grateful.

In the ancient days of the Bible, most Jews were farmers. Like farmers of today the ancient Israelites worried about problems such as enough water and sunshine, disease, or pests that could ruin the crops. They worked very hard to grow and harvest their crops. These ancient Jews lived in villages and walked to the fields each day to tend their crops. The walk from their homes to the fields took a great deal of time and energy. In order to spend more time working in the fields and less on the road, they built small huts near their farms as shelter while they were busy with the harvest. They worked from sunup to sundown and lived in these huts until they had gathered the whole crop. *Sukkah* means hut or booth, and Jews build one now as part of the celebration of this holiday.

The sukkah also reminds Jews of the hut that God told Moses to have the people build when they were wandering in the desert for forty years. These huts provided shelter and protection in the desert. The sukkah that Jewish people build in the yard or at a synagogue is a symbol of those built in the past, and it reminds them that God protects and provides.

The sukkah is not a solid building. Its "walls" are simple upright pieces of lumber or tree branches with cross pieces serving to support the roof. The roof is made from leafy branches that let you see the stars at night. Children like to help build and decorate these festive booths. Decorations can be almost anything you can make. They usually include real fruit, or mobiles made of wax or plastic fruit, paper chains in bright colors, or handdrawn pictures. Today, most Jews do not live in the sukkah, but they do celebrate by eating meals or snacks there.

The holiday of Sukkoth lasts for seven days. Along with the sukkah, two other symbols help Jews celebrate the holi-

*Members of a Jewish youth group
in New York City built their sukkah
on top of an apartment building to
celebrate the holiday Sukkoth.*

day. These are the *etrog* and *lulav*. Both of these are made from special plants. The etrog is a fruit that looks like a large lemon, but the taste is different. It comes from a citron tree and has a special smell. The lulav is made by binding together leaves from palm, myrtle, and willow branches. These two symbols—the etrog and lulav—serve as reminders of the beautiful growing things of the world. They are used in the prayers that are said before eating in the sukkah.

The last day of Sukkoth is different from the rest as it is not festive. This day, which is called Shemini Atzereth, is a day for asking that future harvests be blessed with rain. On this day the etrog and lulav are not waved and there are solemn prayers offered for rain. Farmers always want enough rain for the crops, but in Israel, which is a desert, rain has always been especially important.

TU BI-SHEVAT

In a desert, trees, like rain, are an important resource. They help to prevent soil erosion (soil washing or begin blown away), provide material for shelter, and bear fruit to eat. Trees have always been important to Jews, because Israel is a desert country. This is why they set aside a special day for trees. Tu bi-Shevat, which means the fifteenth day of the month of Shevat, is like a birthday for trees. Tu bi-Shevat is celebrated at the time of year when it is still cold in the United States, but in Israel the air is warming and trees are beginning to get new leaves.

Tu bi-Shevat is a holiday that reminds Jews of Biblical times, when Jews offered fruit from the harvest in praise of God. According to the Torah, people could not eat the fruit of a tree for the first three years. The fourth year the fruit could only be offered in praise of God. From the fifth year on, however, people were permitted to eat the fruit. It was hard to remember which tree was planted in which year, but no one wanted to eat the fruit before the fifth year. To solve this problem, rabbis chose a date that was to be the birthday of the trees and every tree is counted a year older on that day. This day is the fifteenth day of the month of Shevat.

Fruits and nuts that grow on trees such as carobs, almonds, figs, dates, and pomegranates are eaten on this holiday. This custom reminds Jews that trees are necessary if the desert country of Israel is to be kept green and growing.

In Israel, school children celebrate Tu bi-Shevat by planting tiny trees. It is also a custom in Israel to plant a tree for a new child in the family, a cedar tree for a boy and a cypress tree for a girl. At a wedding, branches from the tree of the groom and bride are used to make the wedding canopy under which the couple stand during the ceremony.

Many American Jews contribute money that buys trees to be planted in Israel in honor of a family member, a teacher, or a friend who has died. By buying a tree in Israel, which will carry the name of that person, they also pay honor to trees for their many uses not only in Israel but all over the world.

SHAVUOT

A third harvest holiday is Shavuot. This holiday celebrates the spring harvest of wheat and the first fruits. It also welcomes the coming of summer. As with many Jewish holidays, there is another reason for Shavuot. It marks the day that Jews received the Ten Commandments from God on Mount Sinai.

Shavuot means "weeks." From the day after Passover,

These children in Israel are planting a tree on Tu bi-Shevat.

Jews begin counting seven weeks, which brings them through the spring. Shavuot, the fiftieth day of the count marks the end of those weeks.

The Ten Commandments are the Jews' covenant, or agreement with God. God offered the Jews the commandments, which they agreed to obey and live by in the special ways that are stated in the Torah. The Ten Commandments and Torah are rules from God and are important gifts. Freedom was given to the Jews at Passover, but Shavuot gave the Jews rules to live by as a free people. This holiday celebrates the giving of the Commandments and the way that God and the Jewish people work together.

Thousands of years ago Jews celebrated the first harvest by bringing two loaves of bread and the finest fruits to the Temple in Jerusalem. From all over Israel, farmers and their families joined the parade of people bringing offerings to the Temple. Today, Jews do not offer the harvest to God, but they have developed other customs to celebrate this day and remember God's laws.

In one celebration of Shavuot, some Jews stay up all night in the synagogue studying and reading the Torah together. In the morning Shavuot service, the congregation hears the reading of the Torah portion about the giving of the Ten Commandments. The second portion is the story of Ruth. Ruth was not born a Jew, but she converted to Judaism and followed the Ten Commandments and the customs of the Jewish people. The story of Ruth takes place during the spring harvest. Ruth is the great-grandmother of David who was a great king of Israel. King David died on Shavuot.

In some synagogues it is the custom to hold religious school graduations on this holiday. Students who have completed their studies can now "harvest" or use their knowledge as adults in their communities.

At home, people sometimes decorate the house with branches and fruit. Because Israel is referred to as a land of milk and honey, Jews eat foods made from grain and milk. On Shavuot a favorite of many Jews is cheese-filled crepes called *blintzes.* In Israel, children have parades and carry baskets of fruit. (Another name for Shavuot is Hag Hakikkurim—the Festival of the First Fruits.) Carrying these baskets of fruit is a reminder that the ancient Israelites traveled to Jerusalem to offer thanks to God for the harvest and the Ten Commandments.

4

HISTORICAL
HOLIDAYS

History is the recorded story of true things that happened to people living a long time ago. This chapter tells the story of two important historical events in the history of the Jewish people and how and why these events are celebrated today. We'll look first at Passover; then Shabbat, the Sabbath.

PASSOVER

The name Passover or Pesach, as it is called in Hebrew, comes from the biblical story of the ten plagues. Over 3,000 years ago, the Jews were slaves to the Egyptian Pharaoh, and Moses tried to convince the ruler to let the Jews go free. Pharaoh refused, and so God sent ten plagues on the Egyptians. The last one was the death of the firstborn of every Egyptian family. To make sure that their own children were not killed, the Jews put the blood of a young lamb on their doors. This way God could pass over the homes of the Jews and spare their firstborn children. The last plague finally convinced Pharaoh to free the Jews.

The Passover holiday celebrates the Jewish people's release from slavery and the historical event of leaving Egypt. This leaving is called the Exodus.

Passover is observed for seven or eight days and begins with a special feast called a *seder*. The word seder actually means "order," and this name is used because everything is done in a particular order. The seder, held the first and second night of Passover, is often a time when whole families get together. At the seder it is important to tell all the people, especially the young children, the story of the Exodus. To do this Jews use a book called the *Haggadah* (the word *Haggadah* means "telling" in Hebrew) as a guide for relating the history of the exodus. This book also includes songs, prayers, and the order of the meal. The Haggadah may be written in Hebrew or English and is often beautifully illustrated.

Jews work hard to prepare their houses for Passover and the seders. The house must be clean from attic to basement. It is especially important to make sure that no bits of leavened bread are left in the house.

Any food that rises when it cooks is called leavened food. Ordinary yeast breads, or cakes made with baking powder, are examples of leavened food, which is also called *hametz*. The hametz is removed because the Jews who fled from Egypt at the time of the Exodus did not have time to bake their bread. They left so fast there was no time to let the dough rise and bake in the oven. Instead, they took the dough and put it in the packs they carried on their backs. The hot sun baked the dough into flat unrisen bread called *matzoth*. Throughout the eight days of Passover Jews eat only matzoth and food that has not risen in cooking. The cleaning of the house may include the symbolic use of a feather, a wooden spoon, and a candle to burn the last crumbs of hametz. Children join the parents in this ceremonial burning as they use the feather to sweep the crumbs onto the spoon.

Another part of the seder preparations is to pack up all the everyday dishes and utensils from the kitchen. These are stored, and special Passover ones are placed in the clean kitchen. Next, it is time to prepare the seder itself.

The seder table is set with a fine tablecloth and Passover dishes. On the table is a seder plate containing these items:

zeroa—a roasted shank (leg) bone of a lamb, which is a reminder that God passed over the homes marked with lamb's blood.

betzah—a roasted egg as a symbol of ancient Temple sacrifices. This egg also stands for springtime and the beginning of new life.

maror—a bitter-tasting herb (usually horseradish) to help remember how bitter or terrible it is to be a slave.

haroset—a mixture made of chopped apples, nuts, cinnamon, and wine. This substance looks like mortar, which is used to hold bricks together and is a reminder of the work the Jews did as slaves.

karpas—a green vegetable like parsley is a springtime symbol.

Also on the seder table is saltwater to represent the tears the Jews shed as slaves, a cup of wine for the prophet Elijah,

*This table is elegantly laid for the
seder on the first night of Passover.
Along with the ritual wine and matzah
is a container of salt water and the
seder plate containing the symbolic
foods of the seder—an egg, haroset,
parsley, horseradish, and a lamb shank.*

who you will read more about at the end of the seder, and three layers of matzoth in a cloth case complete the table.

At each place at the seder table there is a cup of wine (children have grape juice), and a Haggadah. The leader's chair has a pillow on it, which serves as a reminder that free people can eat in a reclined position to be comfortable and relaxed.

The ritual of the seder consists of as many as fourteen main parts and can take several hours to complete. Not all Jewish families follow the Haggadah from start to finish, but they usually include the following parts:

After the leader has washed his hands, each person dips the parsley into the saltwater to think of spring, new life, and the sadness of slavery. Then the leader takes the matzoth from inside the middle layer of the matzoth cover and breaks it in half. This is called the *afikomin* and serves as the dessert. The leader will hide the afikomin during the seder when he is required to wash his hands. The children will search for it after they eat the meal. Afikomin customs vary and some families give gifts or money to the children "to buy back" the dessert matzoth.

The youngest child at the seder then asks four questions to find out why Jews celebrate Passover. The answers to the questions tell of the Exodus from Egypt and help everyone to remember that Passover celebrates the freedom from slavery when God led the Jews out of Egypt.

The child wants to know: Why is this night different from all other nights? (This question refers to the seder night.) Question one asks why Jews eat matzoth instead of bread or crackers. Question two seeks to know why Jews eat maror, the bitter herbs. Question three asks why we dip two times.

Question four asks why we eat in a reclining or resting position.

The explanation of the symbols on the seder plate actually answer these questions. To be sure that everyone understands why the seder and Passover are different, the Haggadah continues the explanation.

The ten plagues are listed, and as the leader states each, family members dip a finger in their wine and spill drops of it on their plates as a reminder that the Egyptians had to suffer so the Jewish people could be free.

Finally, the story of the Exodus is recounted. Usually each person recites part of the story as it is written in the Haggadah, sometimes the story is told by song. Four cups of wine are drunk as the story of God's promise is told.

The seder is almost finished when the children open the door to invite the prophet Elijah to come in and join the seder. According to legend, Elijah is the prophet who is supposed to announce the arrival of a new age of peace and joy. The door is opened each year in the hope that Elijah will enter. The last words that are spoken are "Next year in Jerusalem" because not all Jews in the world are free. These words are a prayer for all Jews to be free.

SHABBAT

The Sabbath—Shabbat—is different from the other holidays described in this book and is considered the holiest of holy days. Each of these holidays comes once a year, but the Sabbath is celebrated every week. It is a special day that is called the Shabbat Queen because it is like the arrival of a royal visitor. This queen visits Jewish homes every week and brings feelings of peace and rest.

In the Bible we learn that God made the world in six days. He started with a blank, empty darkness and added something each day. So after creating light and darkness; heaven, earth and ocean; trees and plants; sun, moon, and stars; animals, birds, and fish; and finally, people, He rested.

Just as God looked over His work for the week and rested, Jews, too, make the Sabbath a time to stop all work and look at what they have done. This helps them to see what has been important and to help plan what to do the next week.

Shabbat begins at sundown on every Friday evening. The Sabbath day is Saturday. Jews say goodbye to the Shabbat Queen after sundown Saturday evening. Each of these three times is celebrated by the whole family with special prayers and rituals.

On Friday, the preparations begin for welcoming the Shabbat Queen. The house is cleaned and family members take extra care to be clean and neat to begin the Sabbath supper.

Before the meal is served, the mother lights the Sabbath candles. She waves her hands around the candles and towards her face several times before saying the blessing. The ritual has more than one meaning. The one most often given is that it is a way of welcoming the Sabbath. With her hands in front of her eyes to block out the light from the candles until the blessing has been said, she says this prayer over the Sabbath candles.

Blessed are You, Lord our God, King of all the universe, who has made us holy by giving us His commandments, and has commanded us to kindle the Sabbath lights.

*In this Orthodox family, the mother
lights the Sabbath candles.*

Next, the father says the Kiddush, a prayer over the ritual wine. The best-known portion of the Kiddush prayer is

Blessed are You, Lord our God, King of the universe, who creates the fruit of the vine.

At the end of the Kiddush, everyone takes a sip of the wine. Then one more blessing is given before the family can begin to eat the Shabbat meal. It is the blessing said over the challah, the special loaf of bread that is served on Shabbat and other holidays. The challah loaf looks like it is twisted or braided and is very tasty. It is placed on the table under a cloth called the challah cover. Many families use an embroidered challah cover that is very old and has been passed from one generation to another. Sometimes the cover is one the children made as a project in Hebrew school where they learn about the Jewish faith. When the father uncovers the challah, he says this prayer:

Blessed are You, Lord our God, King of the universe who brings forth bread from the earth.

Everyone repeats this prayer, takes a piece of the challah, and begins the Sabbath meal, which often consists of soup, baked chicken, vegetables, and a noodle pudding. After dinner it is time for the services.

In the synagogue the Friday evening services begin after sundown and the songs and prayers welcome the Sabbath. "Lechah Dodie" is a song that compares the Sabbath to a lovely bride. Everyone in the congregation stands and faces the door of the synagogue to welcome the Sabbath as it comes in the building.

When the Friday evening service is over, the people wish each other a "Shabbat Shalom," a Hebrew expression that means "peaceful Sabbath." Another saying is in Yiddish—"Gut Shabbes," meaning "Good Sabbath."

Saturday is the main day of the Sabbath and is a time to set aside all work and be with God. This means that Jews who observe the Sabbath spend it relaxing, praying, thinking alone, or just being with the family. It is not a day for working, shopping, cooking, traveling, doing housework, going to the movies, or conducting business.

In the morning, people go to the synagogue for Sabbath services. Saturday morning is one of the times during the week that a portion of the Torah is read. During any of these readings boys who are thirteen can read from the Torah. This ceremony is called a Bar Mitzvah. It means that he can assume adult religious responsibilities. Reform and Conservative Jews also include girls in this ceremony (Bat Mitzvah) of becoming an adult. The Bat Mitzvah traditionally takes place on Friday evening. Sometimes parents bring a new baby to be blessed and named, or perhaps a couple who will be married soon come for a pre-wedding blessing.

The afternoon is a time to be with friends to talk or walk outdoors. Even a nap is fine. The Sabbath is time set aside to rest your body from all work.

Even a day as calm and restful as Shabbat must come to an end. Jews say goodbye to Shabbat with another special ceremony called the *Havdalah*. For this ceremony a large twisted candle, a cup of wine, and a besamin box (spice box) are used. The candle is made of several strands of wax braided together; the wine cup is filled to overflowing; and the spice box has holes or windows to let the aroma of fragrant spices fill the room.

First the wine is blessed. These rituals represent the separation between the weekdays and the Sabbath. This separation is voiced in the Havdalah blessing. The first part of the Havdalah blessing says: Blessed are You, Lord our God, King of the Universe, who divides the holy from the ordinary, the light from the darkness.

The ceremony closes this special day of freedom, one in which in the Fourth Commandment God commands Jews to keep: "Observe the Sabbath and keep it holy." If your family observes the Sabbath, they now feel rested and prepared to face all the tasks of the week ahead.

5

FESTIVALS

Festivals are an important part of Jewish life. The meaning of these festivals is celebrated by parades, candlelight, games, picnics, and costumes. The roots of these festivities are found in tradition, legend, and history. This chapter tells how these festival holidays got started and how they are celebrated today.

SIMCHAT TORAH

The day after Sukkoth is the beginning of the Jewish holiday of Simchat Torah, which means "rejoicing for the Torah." It is one of the happiest holidays of the year. The main reason for this joyous holiday is that the Jewish people want to celebrate a book—the Torah.

Each week on Monday, Thursday, and Shabbat a portion or section of the Torah scroll is read aloud in the synagogue. It takes a year to complete the entire scroll. The day that the readings are completed is marked by the holiday of Simchat Torah. Once the readings are completed, it is time to go back to the beginning and start all over. Thus Simchat Torah actually marks the finish and the starting again of the Torah readings.

Jews begin to celebrate this holiday on Simchat Torah eve. Everyone, especially children, goes to the synagogue. The rabbi takes out all the Torahs (usually 4-7 Torahs) and gives each one to a different person. Each person holding a Torah takes a turn leading all the children in a procession or parade through the synagogue. There are seven of these processions, which are called *hakkafah*. Each time, the children march behind the Torah and there is singing and handclapping. The children sometimes make special flags or small scrolls that they carry as they parade around the synagogue. After the celebration, children are given special treats to eat, such as apples and chocolates.

On Simchat Torah day there are more processions. For this is the time when the last chapters of the Torah are read. These chapters are about Moses and the Jews entering the Promised Land of Israel. It is at this time that Moses dies and the Jews mourn his death. This final chapter is both an end and a beginning. It marks the end of Moses's life as a great leader of the Jewish people. It also marks the start of the life of the Jews in their new homes in their own land.

After completing the final reading, it is time to turn to the beginning. The first chapter is about the beginning when God created the world.

As these chapters are being read, a person is called upon to say special blessings, *berachat*, for each section of the readings. One of these blessings is said by children who are younger than twelve or thirteen years of age. They all gather

at the front of the synagogue and stand under a large prayer shawl (tallit). An adult then leads them in the prayers.

It is a special honor to be called to say the blessings on Simchat Torah. That is because the Torah is so important to the Jewish people. It is a special book, but it's also more than a book. It is an agreement with God. The Torah is a history of the Jewish people as well as their law, which tells how Jews should conduct their lives. For all these reasons Jews celebrate the Torah on this festive day. Throughout history oppressors banned the reading of the Torah and thus underlying this holiday is the joy of religious freedom.

CHANUKAH

Another festive occasion that echoes this same theme is the celebration of Chanukah. Many people think this holiday marks a victory in war. However, it really celebrates the re-dedication of the Temple when the battles were over. The story of Chanukah is filled with battles, warriors, miracles, and people who were determined to be free to practice their own religion.

The story of Chanukah begins at the time when King Antiochus of Syria ruled Judea, about 2,500 years ago. At this time Judea was all that remained of the kingdom of Israel after it had been conquered by the Greek ruler Alexander the Great.

On the holiday of Simchat Torah
the Torah scrolls are carried in joyous
procession around the synagogue.

Some Jews enjoyed living like the Greeks and gave up their religious ways. But there were many who continued to live and worship as Jews. King Antiochus wanted to destroy the Jewish religion. He put Greek idols and altars in every town. Jews were ordered to worship these Greek gods and forbidden to practice Judaism.

Mattathias was one Jew who could not follow these rules. He saw a Jew making a sacrifice to a Greek god and became so angry that he killed the man. Fearing for his own life, he fled with his five sons and hid in the mountains. Other Jews who wished to keep their faith joined him, and a small army grew.

When Mattathias died, his son Judah commanded this army. Judah and his soldiers became known as the Maccabees, a word that means hammer, and for three years they fought the Syrians. This was not easy, as the Syrians had more soldiers and better equipment. They even used elephants like tanks to attack the Maccabees. The Jewish soldiers fought a guerrilla style of warfare using unusual methods that often surprised the Syrians. In the American Revolution, the patriots fought this same style of combat against the British. In both cases it was successful. The Maccabees continued to hammer at their Syrian enemies, and eventually defeated them. Now they could enter Jerusalem once again.

Judah marched with his men to the Temple where they tore down the Greek idol of the god Zeus. They cleaned the Temple from top to bottom to make it a place worthy of worshipping God. Legend tells us that as they made ready to light the great lamp (the menorah), which was always kept burning in the Temple, they realized that there was only enough holy oil to burn for one day. Judah sent for more oil, which had to be made from olives. It would take about a week to get it to the Temple. Everyone was worried because the menorah was not supposed to be left unlit. By a miracle, that small bit of oil burned for eight nights, until new oil arrived.

Chanukah celebrates this miracle of the oil and the bravery of the Maccabees. It also celebrates the dedication of the Temple; in fact, the Hebrew word for dedication is *chanukah*.

The Festival of Lights, as Chanukah is also called, is celebrated for eight days. Children eagerly look forward to the special foods and games of this holiday. The house is decorated with colorful Jewish stars, paper chains and pictures. A special candle holder, used only for this holiday, is the Chanukah menorah or *hanukkiah*. There is space for eight separate candles—one for each night the oil burned. To light each candle a helper or servant candle called a *shammash* is used. On the first night of Chanukah one candle is placed in the far right space. The shammash is used to light the candle and blessings are said.

Each night for the next seven nights of Chanukah another candle is added until all eight plus the shammash brighten the house. Songs are sung, "Maoztzur" (Rock of Ages) is a favorite, and the traditional game of *dreidel* may be played. A dreidel is a four-sided top with a Hebrew letter on each side.

The letters on the dreidel stand for Nes Gadol Hayah Sham. The words mean "a great miracle happened there" and refer to the origin of Chanukah. The rules for the dreidel game are found in chapter 7.

Favorite foods served at a Chanukah meal include potato *latkes* which are small fried pancakes made from potatoes,

*A special menorah with eight candles
is used during the celebration of
Chanukah, the Festival of Lights.*

onions, flour, and eggs and served with applesauce as a topping. Israelis and some Americans enjoy *sufganiot*—jelly doughnuts. Both latkes and doughnuts are fried in oil as a reminder of the miracle of the oil that burned for eight nights.

Each night of Chanukah is festive with songs, food, decorations, and candlelight. Another American custom is the giving of gifts each night of Chanukah. The older gift tradition is that of giving Chanukah gelt (money) to children. You can find a newer version of this in stores at Chanukah time each year. Chocolate candy Chanukah gelt is always a welcome present. Also, a modern tradition is giving toys as presents.

A menorah can be any shape as long as it has space for eight candles and a shammash. Some menorahs use oil instead of candles. Chanukah is usually celebrated in the winter and the lights of the candles brighten the dark nights. You can see a giant menorah in Washington, D.C. in a park called the Ellipse, which is across from the White House. Each year the President and members of the Jewish community light the electric lights of the menorah.

LAG BA OMER

An *omer* is the bundle of barley that was brought to the Temple in ancient days. From the second day of Passover until the holiday of Shavuot, fifty days are counted. During this time the ancient Jewish farmers of Israel quietly watched over their crop of wheat. This was an anxious time because a poor wheat crop meant hunger and even starvation. This fifty day period was one in which there were only quiet and tense days. Only the thirty-third day—Lag ba Omer—is an exception. This holiday started in the days of the Romans. Once again the Jews were conquered and Judea was ruled by the Romans. Again Jews were forbidden to practice their religion. One teacher refused to obey the Romans and fled to the hills of Galilee where he lived with his youngest son in a cave for thirteen years. He was Rabbi Simeon ben Yohai. Every year on the thirty-third day of Omer, his former students came to the hills to hear him speak.

Another Jew who disobeyed the Roman law was Rabbi Akiva. He knew the Roman emperor would not let him teach the Torah so he devised a plan to outwit him. He asked his students to act as if they were going on a hunting picnic and the Roman guards let them go out to the fields. There Akiva would meet them and teach the Torah.

Today, Lag ba Omer is celebrated by school children as a special day for a picnic. In Israel it is a festive day of dancing and picnicking and remembering some very wise leaders.

PURIM

The story behind the holiday of Purim is found in the Scroll of Esther—Megillat Esther. It is a holiday that is a special favorite of children. It is the time for merrymaking that includes dressing up in costumes. Children are even encouraged to make as much noise as possible. Tasty pastries called *hamantaschen* are eaten during this holiday.

The origins of Purim are not very clear. Most historians agree, however, that the events took place in Persia (now Iran) during the reign of King Ahasuerus about 2,500 years ago. His wife, Queen Vashti, once refused to appear at a banquet and the king became so angry at her disobedience that he had her killed. He then began a search for a new queen.

The king chose a beautiful young woman named Esther. Esther was Jewish, but the king didn't know this. Her faith will become an important fact later in the story.

A favorite advisor of the king was a vain man named Haman. Haman hated the Jews of Persia because they would not bow down to him. Jews do not bow down to men, only God, but Haman felt they should bow down to him. One man in particular refused to bow to Haman. His name was Mordecai and he was Esther's uncle.

The king also knew Mordecai. In fact, Mordecai had once saved the king's life. King Ahasuerus planned to honor Mordecai for this act of bravery and asked Haman to suggest a way to honor an important man. Haman thought the king meant to honor him, and he suggested a very grand honor. Haman proposed that the man be dressed in the king's clothes, be seated on the king's horse, and be led through the streets by the king's man. Haman was furious when he realized that it would actually be Mordecai who would be honored and Haman would lead the horse!

Haman's determination to kill the Jews grew and he approached the king with cunning lies about the Jews of Persia. The lies convinced the king and he gave Haman permission to carry out his plan. The date for the destruction of the Jews was decided by a lottery. (Purim means casting lots or lottery.) The thirteenth day of the month Adar was the date drawn in the lottery. Adar is the twelfth month of the Jewish calendar and usually falls in February or March.

Mordecai learned of the plan and informed Esther, telling her that she could save the Jews by telling the king that she, too, would be killed if Haman's plan was carried out. This was not an easy task, as even the queen could not ask for an audience with the king, but had to wait until he wished to

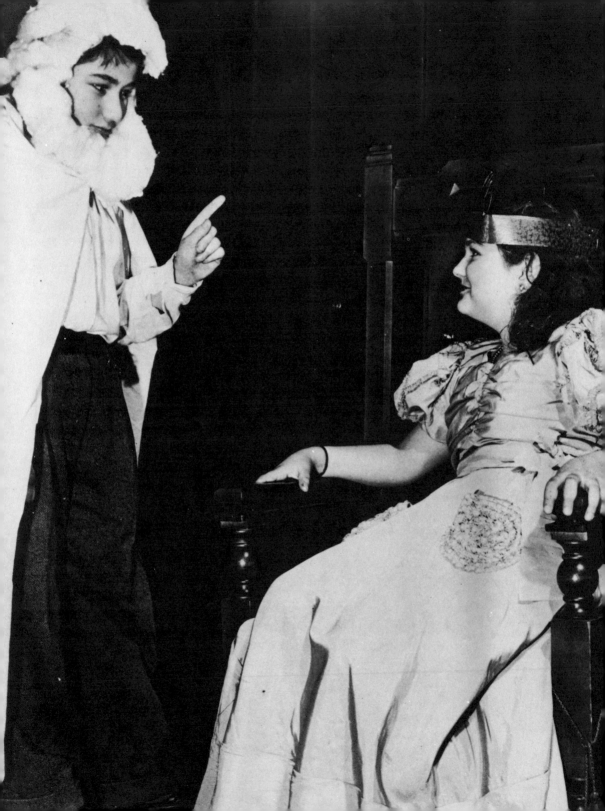

speak to her. Esther had to decide if she should risk her life and position to save the Jews.

Legend says that Esther fasted to help clear her mind so that she might know what to do. She decided to invite the king to a party so that she could speak to him. At the party, Esther told the king that she, too, was a Jew and would be killed if Haman wasn't stopped. The king was impressed with Esther's courage and pride in her people. He ordered that the Jews not be destroyed, and he arrested Haman. Then he made Mordecai his chief advisor and Haman was hanged. The legend explains that Haman had built a gallows that he planned to use to hang Mordecai. The story ends with the Jews being saved and Haman being hanged on his own gallows.

Today, Jews celebrate Purim by reading the scroll of Esther in the synagogue. The first blessing said on Purim is for reading the Megillah (scroll). It thanks God and praises Him for commanding the Jews to read the story of Esther. To stamp out the name of Haman, the children are given noise-makers called *gragers* (pronounced groggers.) They listen carefully to the reader and each time Haman's name is mentioned they shake the gragers.

Religious schools usually plan a day of costume parades, megillah readings, and party atmosphere to celebrate this holiday. Also, teachers emphasize the questions that the sto-

*Purim is often celebrated by plays
in which children take the roles of
Esther and Mordecai whose story
is remembered on this holiday.*

ry of Esther raises. For example, they ask how are minorities treated now? Can Judaism survive outside Israel? What role do women play in the history of the Jewish people? Should Jews attack an enemy if they suspect that an enemy plans to harm them? The stories associated with Purim cannot answer these questions, but the holiday does provide an opportunity to examine how individuals might answer them.

At home, children prepare for Purim by baking hamantaschen and making costumes. Hamantaschen are shaped like three-cornered pockets and are usually filled with a tasty mix of poppy seeds, cherries, prunes, and other fruits. Favorite costumes usually feature one of the people from the story of Esther. Another activity for Purim is making *shalkhmones* baskets, which are given to friends or poor people in the community. These baskets contain fruit, hamantaschen, and small handmade gifts.

6

MODERN HOLIDAYS

So far you have read about holidays commemorating historical events, but the Jewish people have four holidays that memorialize events that have happened in the last fifty years. You will read about the days set aside for remembering these events in this chapter. We begin with the day that recalls the terrible price Jews paid to Nazi Germany.

YOM HASHOAH

The name Yom Hashoah means "day of the whirlwind." This special day helps Jews remember the tragedy of the Holocaust when Jews were the special enemy of Adolf Hitler. A holocaust is the total destruction of something or of a group of people. Hitler's Nazi government forced the Jews to live inside fenced-off areas called ghettos. This separation of the Jews from the other people of Germany wasn't enough for the Nazis, and the next step was to pass laws that

]45[

were harder for the Jews to follow. Finally, Hitler put all the Jews he could find into prisons called concentration camps. Here Jews worked like slaves and were treated cruelly. Some concentration camps were called death camps because the Nazis killed the Jews in these camps. Six million Jews died in the Nazi Holocaust. They were not soldiers but they were shot, gassed, or starved to death because they were Jews. Jews were not the only enemy of Hitler and the Nazis, but they were the largest single group of people that Hitler tried to destroy.

On Yom Hashoah, Jews remember these horrors and realize that sometimes people can be very evil. But it's not a time to feel hopeless either. We remember that some people were brave and tried to help Jews to escape. We also hope that such evil will never strike again.

To celebrate Yom Hashoah many synagogues and religious schools hold serious assemblies to tell about the Holocaust. During the assembly, candles are often lit to honor and remember those millions of people who died. Those who fought against Hitler are also honored. Poems written by children who were in concentration camps are sometimes read to show that even young people perished needlessly. The poems are often sad and full of darkness. Yet between the lines you can hear the hope and faith of the young poets call out.

Another way that Jews all over the world remember the Holocaust is through special prayer services on Yom Hashoah. Again, mourning candles may be lit and a prayer of mourning, the Kaddish, is said for the six million Jews who died.

Of the Jews who lived through the Holocaust, many came to America after World War II ended. Still others went to Palestine to help build the nation that was soon to become Israel.

YOM HA'ATZMA'UT

The celebration of Yom Ha'atzma'ut is in honor of the creation of the free nation of Israel as a homeland for the Jewish people. Yom Ha'atzma'ut is Israel's Fourth of July. In the United States, we celebrate the anniversary of our nation's independence by having a national holiday. It is festive and happy, and people enjoy going to see the fireworks. These celebrations have been going on for over two hundred years. The tiny country of Israel is so new that you probably know people who can remember when it was created. In the year 1948, Israel became a nation. Is this country much older than you?

We know that the nation of Israel existed in the Bible and that Jews lived there and practiced their religion. But large armies conquered the Jews and took them as slaves or scattered them throughout the Middle East. For 2,000 years there was no Jewish homeland called Israel. In fact, the Hebrew language wasn't spoken as a language except in the synagogues by people who used it in prayers. Some Jews were able to remain in the land that was once Israel, but it was always ruled by another, larger nation or empire.

About one hundred years ago a group of Jews from Russia decided to return to their ancient homeland and try to live there. The land was called Palestine then and there were both Arabs and Jews living there. The land was mostly desert and hard to farm. Making a living was hard and most of the people there were very poor. As more people came to Palestine as pioneers, they brought better ideas for watering or irrigating the crops. Soon, farming began to flourish and towns were built.

One person well known for his work in encouraging Jews to become pioneer settlers in Palestine is Theodor Herzl. He believed that it was important for the Jewish people to be able to have their own country or homeland. He worked for many years to get other people to share his dream. This belief in a separate homeland for Jews is called Zionism. People who agreed with Herzl believed in returning to Palestine and creating a Jewish homeland. But Palestine didn't belong to the Jews at that time. It was part of the Turkish empire until the end of World War I, and after that it became part of the British empire.

While there were many Jews living in Palestine who wanted a homeland, there were also many Arabs who claimed the land was theirs. Who should have it? Fighting broke out as each side tried to keep their homeland. Finally, in 1947 the United Nations decided to establish two countries. One would be the Jewish state of Israel; the other, a country for the Arabs of Palestine. On May 14, 1948 the state of Israel became a free nation.

Nationhoud caused great joy throughout the world as Jews from every country rejoiced in the creation of their homeland. Nowhere was the happiness greater than in Israel itself. People danced in the streets and sang songs of joy. This happiness was soon turned into sorrow as the Arab enemies of the new state declared war the next day.

After many months of fighting, the Arabs agreed to end the war. When the fighting stopped, Israel had doubled its size, taking in all the territory the United Nations had assigned to the Arabs. This resulted in increased tension between Israel and the Arab countries. War broke out in 1956, 1967, and again in 1973. But Israel survived as an independent nation and as the only democracy in the Middle East.

Since Israel is a Jewish nation, all the Jewish holidays are national holidays. The language of the country is Hebrew, which was brought back to life with the creation of Israel. New words had to be created to explain all the things that had come into being in the world since the last time Hebrew was an everyday language. There were no words for things like television, cars, computers, even bicycles.

In Israel, the day of Independence is celebrated by parades and special events. Sometimes Air Force planes fly overhead. Everyone has a holiday. People sing and dance up and down the streets of every city in Israel. Television and radio programs offer special concerts and biographies of famous Jewish leaders.

In the United States, Jewish children celebrate Israel's Independence Day with assemblies and parties in religious schools. Children make crafts projects on Israeli themes. They make Israeli flags and maps. Often they learn Israeli songs and dances. Special treats might include foods that are popular in Israel today.

YOM YERUSHALAYIM

Israel's war of independence was a hard war. The Israeli fighters had few guns and not enough equipment. Their Arab enemies captured part of Jerusalem and this old city became divided. A barbed wire fence, guarded by armed soldiers, ran through the city. Jews were allowed to live as they

In Israel, Independence Day is
marked by festive street dances.

wished on their side of the fence. But a very holy place for Jews was located in the Arab half of Jerusalem. This place is called the Western Wall. It is special to Jews because it is part of the remains of the first Temple built in Jerusalem.

In 1967, war once again broke out between Israel and the Arab countries. This time the Israeli army was better prepared and won the war in six days. In this Six Day War the Israeli army captured the other half of Jerusalem. The city remains under Jewish control today.

The holiday of Yom Yerushalayim was created to celebrate the unification of Jerusalem. It is celebrated on the twenty-eighth day of the Jewish month of Iyor. Every year on this day the people of Israel rejoice in parades through the streets of Jerusalem.

YOM HAZIKKARON

Another modern holiday is Yom Hazikkaron, which means "Remembrance Day." On this day Israelis remember all the men and women who have died fighting for Israel. It is a solemn day that is celebrated the day before Independence Day. In Israel, many people visit a military cemetery to mourn those who were killed in battle. The Israeli flag is flown at half mast in their honor. Schools, synagogues, army camps, and military cemeteries also hold memorial services.

A siren blows early in the morning to start this sad day and it is followed by two minutes of silence throughout the country. When the first stars appear at night, another siren signals the solemn day is over, and the day to celebrate Independence Day has begun.

THE IMPORTANCE
OF HOLIDAYS

We began this book with an introduction to the kinds of holidays Jews celebrate. Now that you have found out more about them you see that these holidays, like those in every large society, serve the needs of people. Every group needs some way of remembering their past and some way of keeping people together. And, of course, ways have to be found to teach young people the knowledge of their heritage and of their faith. The Jewish holidays fill all of these needs. Through them the Jewish people learn how to keep their past and to provide for the future.

7

HOLIDAY RECIPES AND CRAFTS

Cooking and baking special treats for Jewish holidays can make the holidays more fun. Most of them can be made from the materials you have in your home.

One part of a traditional meal served in Sephardic homes (Spanish and Mid-Eastern background) for Shavuot are cheese pastries, called Sembussak. Here's how you make them.

SEMBUSSAK

For the pastry you need:
2 cups flour
2 ½ sticks of butter (room temp.)
¼ to ½ cup warm water
1 cup smead (semolina)
¼ teaspoon salt
2 ounces sesame seeds

For the filling:
2 lbs grated Muenster cheese
2 eggs beaten

Pastry Mix
Mix flour, smead, salt, butter together in a large bowl. Add a little water at a time. Mix until well blended. Cover and set aside.

Filling
Combine cheese and beaten eggs. Mix lightly.

Now you are ready to make the shells and fill them.

1. Preheat the oven to 350°F.
2. Make ping pong size balls out of the dough.
3. Dip one side of each ball in the sesame seeds.
4. Flatten each ball to a circle about 2½" in diameter (The seeds should be on the bottom of the circle.)
5. Place 1 tsp. of filling in the center of each circle.
6. Fold to make a half moon shape with the seeds covering the outside.
7. Pinch to close ends firmly.
8. Bake on ungreased cookie sheet at 350° for 15 minutes or until lightly browned. Do not overbake or the seeds will burn.
9. Serve hot.

HAMANTASCHEN
(3 dozen)

5½ cups flour
4 eggs

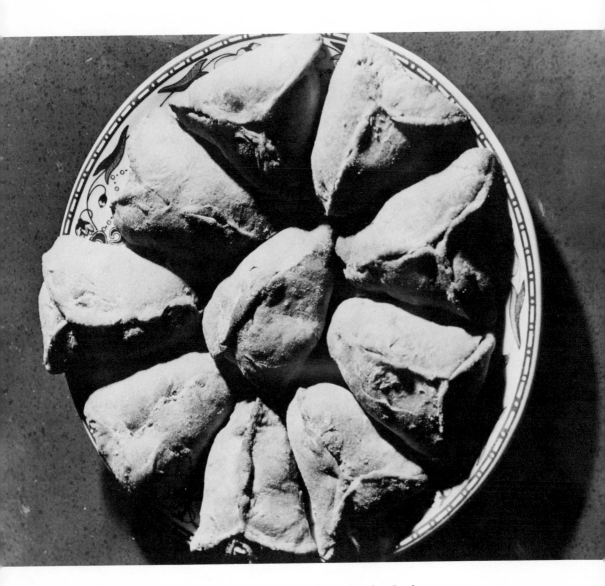

Hamantaschen are a favorite food of
the Purim holiday celebration.

1 cup cooking oil
1½ cups sugar
2 tablespoons vanilla
2 tablespoons baking powder
1 jar (6 ounces) of preserves (any flavor)

1. Preheat oven to 350°.
2. Combine the oil, sugar, eggs, vanilla, baking powder in a large bowl. Mix well.
3. Add the flour a little at a time.
4. Beat the mixture until well blended.
5. Lightly flour a board or kitchen countertop.
6. Roll out the dough ¼ inch thick on the floured surface.
7. Cut circles 2 inches in diameter in the dough with a knife or cookie cutter.
8. Put circles on a greased and lightly floured cookie sheet. Spoon ½-1 teaspoon preserves in the center of each.
9. Make three pinches in the dough to form a triangle.
10. Bake at 350°F for 30 minutes. Cool before serving.

(Note: If dough is too sticky, add flour by tablespoon until the mixture doesn't stick to your fingers.)

EASY NO-FLOUR PASSOVER COOKIES

1 cup sugar
2 egg whites
2 cups ground walnuts or almonds

1. Pre-heat oven to 350°
2. Mix all ingredients together.

3. Drop the dough by teaspoonsful on a cookie sheet that has been lined with aluminum foil.
4. Bake at 325° for 15-20 minutes
5. Cool

EASY CHALLAH
(*makes 2 loaves*)

2 eggs
5 cups flour
¼ cup oil
3 tsp salt
1½ packages of dry yeast
  (¼ ounce each package)
¼ cup sugar

1. Preheat oven to 350°
2. Put the flour in a large bowl.
3. Make a hole or well in the middle of the flour.
4. Put oil, eggs, salt in the well.
5. Dissolve the yeast in a cup of warm water.
6. Put sugar in the yeast and mix well.
7. Add yeast and sugar mix to flour and blend.
8. Knead this dough mixture. Add water if needed.
9. Divide the dough in half to make two loaves. Divide each half into three parts and shape each part into a long roll.
10. For each loaf, braid three lengths of dough as you would a pigtail and tuck the ends in neatly.
11. Let the braided loaves rise for 1 hour.
12. Brush top of each loaf with a beaten egg.
13. Bake at 350° until brown.
    (Check every 10 minutes.)

DREIDEL GAME
For two or more players

The dreidel game is a traditional game played during Chanukah. A dreidel is a four-sided top that can be purchased in many department or novelty stores during the Chanukah season. Each side is marked with a Hebrew letter and each letter stands for an amount in the game. (See diagram, page 60.)

To start the game each player is given 10 coins or nuts and he puts 3 of them into the middle of a circle. This is called the "pot." Now each player spins the dreidel in turn. The letter that lands up when the dreidel stops spinning tells the directions for the player. He must do nothing, take all the pot, take half the pot, or put one of his own pile into the pot. Each time a whole pot is taken, the game starts over. The winner is the one with the most or the only one who is not wiped out!

PAPER MACHE FRUIT

Paper mache fruit are good decorations for a sukkah. You can also use these fruits to decorate the table or your home anytime. Try putting them on strings to make a mobile or hang them one by one. They also look nice in a bowl as a centerpiece.

You will need:
    balloons
    Vaseline
    newspaper and paper towels
    paste (like school paste)
    paint
    large bowl

A nineteenth-century wooden dreidel from Eastern Europe

 nun – wins nothing

 gimmel – wins everything in the "pot" (middle)

 hay – wins half of the "pot"

 shin – puts one into the pot

Directions
1. Blow up a balloon to the size and shape of each fruit. Example: banana, orange, apple, grapefruit.
2. Cover each lightly with Vaseline.
3. Put paste in bowl.
4. Rip newspapers or paper towels into 1 inch wide strips. Dip one at a time in the paste and cover the balloon. Do a layer of towel then newspaper and repeat each layer three times.
5. Let the fruit dry for a day or two.
6. Paint the form to look like the actual fruit. Let dry.
7. Now use a needle and thread (if you need help, ask an adult) to make the mobile or individual hanging fruit.

PURIM GRAGER

To make this noisemaker you need:
    a clean, dry, empty frozen juice can
    a rubber band
    a piece of aluminum foil, folded to
      wrap over the end of the can
    pebbles or dry peas
    scissors, construction paper, crayons, tape,
      other materials for decoration.

Directions:
1. Put about ¼ cup of pebbles or peas in the can.
2. Cover the open end with the foil and wrap the rubber band around it to keep the foil in place.
3. Cut the paper to fit the can.
4. Decorate the paper.
5. Tape it over the can.
6. Shake for noise effect.

TERRARIUM

A popular project for Tu bi-Shevat is making a terrarium. Since most of us will not be able to plant a tree, we can plant some seeds instead.

You will need:
   parsley seeds
   plastic cup (for a larger plant try a fish bowl)
   dirt or potting soil
   plastic wrap, rubber band

Directions:
1. Put potting soil or dirt into the cup until it is ⅔ full.
2. Use your finger to make a hole in the middle for the seeds.
3. Put several seeds into the hole and cover them.
4. Water until the soil is slightly wet ½ way down.
5. Wrap a piece of plastic wrap on the top of the cup and secure with rubber band.
6. Put in a sunny spot for 2 or 3 days
7. Uncover and water again. Cover.
8. Repeat 6 or 7 times until the seeds grow.

Now leave it uncovered until the parsley grows. You can do this project with other herbs, too.

FOR
FURTHER READING

Adler, David A. *A Picture Book of Jewish Holidays.* New York: Holiday House, 1981.
Each holiday is simply explained by a poem and excellent illustrations.

Bernstein, Philip S. *What the Jews Believe.* New York: Farrar, Straus and Giroux, 1950.
This book gives a summary of the beliefs and practices of Jews. It also compares these beliefs with those of the Christian religion.

Bishop, Claire H. *Twenty and Ten.* New York: Penguin Books, Inc., 1978.
A group of French schoolchildren hide ten Jewish children from German soliders.

Eisenberg, Phyllis R. *A Mitzvah Is Something Special.* New York: Harper & Row, 1978.

Lisa is a young girl trying to do something special for both of her grandmothers. In the process, she comes to understand how much the two different grandmothers love her.

Kerr, Judith. *When Hitler Stole Pink Rabbit.* New York: The Putnam Publishing Group, 1972.
Anna's family flees Germany before the situation can get any worse. They make their way through Switzerland and France and finally find freedom in England.

Singer, Isaac Bashevis. *When Shlemiel Went to Warsaw & Other Stories.* New York: Farrar, Straus and Giroux, 1968.
These eight stories are taken from traditional Jewish stories and include humor, fantasy, and even witchery.

Volavkova, Hana. *I Never Saw Another Butterfly: Children's Drawings and Poems from Terezin Concentration Camp, 1942-1944.* New York: Schocken Books, Inc., 1976.
Even in the midst of death, children aspire for love, freedom, peace and hope.

Voss, Carl Hermann. *Living Religions of the World: Our Search for Meaning.* Cleveland and New York: Excalibur Books, The World Publishing Company, 1968.
A brief and clear explanation of the world's great religions, including their origins, history, and beliefs.

INDEX

Abraham, 6–7
Alenu prayer, 6
Arabs, 48–49, 51
Ashkenazim, 4

Bar Mitzvah, 30
Bat Mitzvah, 30
Bible, 2, 14, 27, 47

Calendar, Jewish, 2–3, 5
Challah, 8, 29, 57
Chanukah, 35–39
Children, 9, 12, 14, 22, 23, 25, 33, 39, 40, 43, 44, 49
Conservative Jews, 4
Crafts, 3, 4, 37, 44, 58–62

David, King, 19
Dreidel game, 37, 58, 59

Egypt, 21–26
Elijah, 23, 26
Esther, 40–44

Etrog, 16
Exodus, 22, 25, 26

Fasting, 8, 9, 12
Festival Holidays, 2, 32–44
Foods, 3, 4, 8, 12, 20, 22–25, 29, 37, 39, 44, 53–57

Greeks, 35–36

Haggadah, 22, 25, 26
Hamantaschen (recipe), 54–56
Harvest Holidays, 2, 13–20
Havdalah, 30–31
Herzl, Theodor, 48
High Holy Days, 2, 5–12
Historical Holidays, 2, 21–31

Importance of holidays, 52
Independence Day, 49–51
Israel, 47–51

Jerusalem, 3, 20, 49, 51

Kaddish, 46
Kiddush prayer, 29
Kol Nidre prayer, 9

Lag ba Omer, 39–40
Lulav, 16

Matzoth, 22, 25
Menorah, 37–39
Modern Holidays, 2, 45–52
Mordecai, 41–43
Moses, 2, 14, 21, 33

Nazi Germany, 45–46

Orthodox Jews, 4, 28, 30

Palestine, 47–48
Paper mache fruit, 58, 60
Passover, 17, 19, 21–26
Passover cookies (recipe), 56–57
Persia, 40–41
Purim, 40–44, 55
Purim grager, 61

Recipes, 53–57
Reform Jews, 4, 30
Romans, 40

Rosh Hashanah, 3, 5–8, 11, 12
Rosh Hodesh, 3
Ruth, 19

Sabbath, 26–31
Seder, 22–26
Sembussak (recipe), 53–54
Sephardim, 4, 53
Shammash, 37, 39
Shavuot, 17–20, 53
Shemini Atzereth, 16
Shofar, 6–7, 9–12
Simchat Torah, 32–35
Six Day War, 51
Sukkoth, 13–16, 34, 58

Tashlich, 7
Ten Commandments, 17, 19, 20
Terrarium, 62
Torah, 1, 2, 6–7, 16, 19, 30, 32–35
Tu bi-Shevat, 16–17, 62

Yom Ha'atzma'ut, 47–49
Yom Hashoah, 45–47
Yom Hazikkaron, 51
Yom Kippur, 3, 5, 6, 8–12
Yom Yerushalayim, 49–51